10/07

Life Cycle of an Apple

Apple

Angela Royston

First published in Great Britain by Heinemann Library
Halley Court, Jordan Hill, Oxford OX2 8EJ,
a division of Reed Educational and Professional Publishing Ltd.

Heinemann is a registered trademark of Reed Educational and Professional
Publishing Limited.

Oxford   Melbourne   Auckland   Kuala Lumpur   Singapore
Ibadan   Nairobi   Kampala   Johannesburg   Gaborone
Portsmouth NH (USA)   Chicago

Designed by Celia Floyd
Illustrations by Alan Fraser
Printed in Hong Kong / China

02
10 9 8 7 6 5 4 3

ISBN 0 431 08369 X

British Library Cataloguing in Publication Data

Royston, Angela
Life cycle of an apple
1. Apples – Juvenile literature
I. Title II. Apple
583.7'3

Acknowledgements

The Publisher would like to thank the following for permission to reproduce
photographs:
A–Z Botanical Collection Ltd/F Merlet pgs 7, 8; Bruce Coleman Ltd/Christer
Fredriksson pg 19; Harry Smith Collection pg 24; Holt Studios International/Inga
Spence pgs 5, 18, Holt Studios International/Nigel Cattlin pgs 6, 13; NHPA/David
Woodfall pg 11, NHPA/Stephen Dalton pg 12; Oxford Scientific/Terry Heathcote
pg 4, Oxford Scientific/D R Specker pg 16, Oxford Scientific/Carson Baldwin jr
pgs 20, 26-27; Roger Scruton pgs 9, 10, 14, 15, 17, 21, 22, 23, 25.

Cover photograph: Trevor Clifford/Trevor Clifford Photography.

Our thanks to Dr John Feltwell, Wildlife Matters Consultancy, for his comments in
the preparation of this edition.

Contents

What is an apple?

An apple is a fruit that grows on a tree. There are thousands of different kinds of apple trees. These crab apples taste very **sour**.

late winter

early spring

1 week later

The apples in this book are Red Delicious. They taste sweet and juicy. Every year each tree produces a new crop of apples.

spring

4 weeks later

summer

Late winter

These apple trees are about ten years old. The trees have no leaves and are resting during the cold months of winter.

late winter

early spring

I week later

Each **twig** is covered with tight buds. As the days get a bit warmer, the **buds** begin to open.

spring

4 weeks later

summer

Early spring

Inside the **bud** are tiny leaves. They push through the bud and grow bigger. Soon the whole tree is covered with leaves.

late winter

early spring

I week later

Leaves use water from the soil, sunlight and air to make food for the tree. Pink buds are growing among the leaves.

spring

4 weeks later

summer

Spring

One by one the pink **buds** open out into small pinkish-white flowers. Each flower has five petals with yellow **stamens** in the centre.

late winter

early spring

I week later

Now the whole tree is covered with **blossom**. The flowers smell sweet and the **stamens** are covered in a yellow dust called **pollen**.

spring

4 weeks later

summer

A few days later

This honey bee is flying from flower to flower. It collects **pollen** and stores it on sticky hairs on its back legs.

late winter

early spring

1 week later

Some of the **pollen** from one flower rubs off onto the centre of the next flower. This pollen helps to make tiny apple seeds.

spring

4 weeks later

summer

4 weeks later

The flower has done its job. The petals **wither** and fall off, leaving a tiny apple with the apple seeds inside.

late winter

early spring

1 week later

The apples begin to swell and grow. The skin becomes waxy and shiny, but you can still see the remains of the petals at one end.

spring

4 weeks later

summer

Late spring

This is the caterpillar of a codling moth. It is just one of many insects that likes to eat the leaves and fruit of the apple trees.

late winter

early spring

1 week later

A caterpillar has eaten a hole in this apple. Most farmers spray their trees to kill the insects before they damage the fruit.

spring

4 weeks later

summer

Summer

All summer the apples grow bigger and sweeter. These big red apples are now sweet and **ripe**.

late winter

early spring

I week later

The whole tree is covered with juicy, red apples.

spring

4 weeks later

summer

Early autumn

The apples are picked by hand
and stored carefully in big boxes.
If they are kept cool, they will last
all winter.

late winter

early spring

I week later

Some of the apples fall to the ground before they are picked. Wasps and birds feed on the sweet **flesh** and the apples slowly rot.

spring

4 weeks later

summer

Mid to late autumn

22

The apple trees are getting ready for winter. The leaves turn red and fall to the ground. As they rot, they slowly become part of the soil.

late winter   early spring   I week later

Buds have formed on the **twigs**. They will stay like this until next spring when they will open up into new leaves.

spring

4 weeks later

summer

Winter

Farmers **prune** the trees every winter. They cut off some of the branches to make the tree stronger.

late winter   early spring   I week later

The brown pips inside each apple
are seeds. If they are planted, they
might grow into new apple trees
next spring.

spring

4 weeks later

summer

An apple orchard

This **orchard** produces thousands of **ripe** apples each year. Some will be sold to shops and markets. The rest will be made into pies or juice.

Apple trees start to make fruit at 3 to 5 years. Most farmers usually replace their trees before they are 20 years old.

Life cycle

Late winter

Early spring

I week later

Spring

4 weeks later

Summer

Fact file

People have been eating apples for over 2 million years.

Apple trees only produce good fruit in places that have a cold winter.

We can eat apples all year round, because some countries have their autumn when we have our spring.

One apple tree may produce about 200 apples each year.

In a garden, some apple trees may live for up to 100 years.

Glossary

blossom a mass of flowers on a fruit tree

bud a swelling on a stem that will grow into leaves or a flower

flesh the juicy part of a fruit

orchard a field or garden where fruit trees are grown

pollen the tiny male seeds of a plant

prune to cut back a tree or plant to make it stronger and healthier

ripe fully grown and ready to eat

sour having an acid taste

stamens the parts of a flower that produce male seeds

twig a thin branch

wither to dry up and die

Index